Endorsements

The poetry that Phyllis shares in this book is incredibly touching and profound. She is honest and vulnerable as she continuously balances the goodness and greatness of God that is on display for all to see with the disappointments, fears, and limitations with which she struggles. This is a book of poems that describe the inescapable tension between the way things are and the way things should be . . . and will one day be.

Sharon McCarter, Associate Pastor
Maryville Vineyard Church

Phyllis, your poems are very touching and have a way of visually expressing the world around us. It's exciting to see how God has blessed your writing abilities. I can't help but think about Grandma DeBoer writing short stories and her book. How proud she must be in heaven, having you follow in her footsteps writing poems and stories. Keep on writing!

Gary L. DeBoer, Author's Cousin and Poet
Engineering/Quality Tech Service Manager

In collected "poetic thoughts" that celebrate the natural universe, Phyllis Dolislager chronicles her years-long recurrent and unpredictable physical condition with resounding faith and seemingly endless courage.

As her poetic expressions move through the major themes of nature, faith, life, and health, Dolislager's soul-deep experiences of recurring miracles ("God-things") punctuate her journey through the seasons of her condition. Dolislager finds solace and inspiration in everyday natural occurrences; she finds hope and delight in the smallest signs of life, like the strong green plants that grow relentlessly through cracks in a rock.

Dolislager's struggle to understand and accept her personal condition has elicited poetic responses that continue to encourage and inspire.

Gail Powell, Ph.D.
Language and Literature

More Endorsements

Each of Phyllis' poems captures the essence of a moment, providing a snapshot into our lives through her own. Those things which collectively we treasure most – namely life, health, faith, and nature – are pondered and painted and unwrapped for us in delightfully complex and profoundly simple ways. A wonderful, poignant collection!

Linda Gullufsen,
Author and Composer

Phyllis' poetry is genuine and insightful into daily living. She inspires me to laugh at myself, give thanks, and to see the beauty in all things.

Robin Bailey Macqueen, Chair Authors' Row
Reading Rocks in Rockford

I found the book very interesting especially the parts about the mountains of Tennessee. The verbal picture of the beauty of the Smokies was very moving. Faith and Health have a more personal feel, and they are colored by the personal experience of the reader. Over all very nice work.

Alan Johnson, M.D.
Clinical Professor of Pediatrics
UCSF School of Medicine

This delightful book of poetry speaks straight to the heart as the author shares her inspirational journey through the beauties of nature and her deep faith in God's covering grace for our human frailties. Her lyrical words are a testament to the strength and renewal given to those who place their trust in Christ's ever abiding love.

Jean E. Holmes, Past National President
The National League of American Pen Women

Poetic Thoughts

Nature • Faith • Life • Health

by
Phyllis Porter Dolislager

Creative Consultant: Marsha Lindenschmidt

My Mother Is a Poem

My mother is a role model,
who sets the standards high.
She reaches out to others.
She's generous with her time and money.

She gives advice when asked—
and sometimes "just for free."
But she can be stubborn
when she's on the receiving end.

As we both grow older
we need each other more and more.
It's easier to say, "I love you,"
and to identify the values that we share.

Some days Mother is a "crazy lady,"
other days she's a traditionalist.
But she never fails to have some fun.
I hope I grow old just like her.

5/07

For

My Mother

Eleanor Porter Grifhorst

In honor of her 90th birthday!

Printed in the United States of America
Published by CreateSpace.com

Unless otherwise indicated, all Scripture quotations are from The Holy Bible,
English Standard Version® (ESV®), copyright © 2001 by Crossway,
a publishing ministry of Good News Publishers.
Used by permission. All rights reserved.

ISBN: 13: 978-1479195695
10: 1479195693

To purchase other books by the author,
visit byphyllis.com ~ amazon.com ~ smashwords.com

Preface

Returning from trips with my husband Ron into the Great Smoky Mountain National Park, these colorful word pictures seemed to flow from my mind out onto the page. The mountains were so alive that I started to imagine their human characteristics. It was as if my brain sighed with relief, forgot the everyday stressors, and became creative. When spring arrived, I viewed the budding trees and flowers as part of a fashion show weaving its way into town.

Prior to this, when the weakness of post-polio seemed to hold me captive, I started writing poetry. It gave me the freedom to share my thoughts, my fears, my anxieties. Free verse allowed me to speak boldly and honestly. It was a creative release for me.

This concise style of writing helps me put into plain words not only joy, but sorrow, and also a new way to praise God. I can echo back to Him my admiration of the beauty I see all around me in His creation.

My neighbor, Marsha Lindenschmidt, is an artist, and our granddaughter, Carolina Dolislager, is one of her students. Having their expertise for creative input and various illustrations and having Ron for the formatting made this book a reality.

As you read these *Poetic Thoughts*, I hope you will experience what I saw . . . and sense what I felt.

A Word of Thanks

A special thanks to those who read all of my poems and helped me decide which ones to include in this book.

Darcia Kelley   Helen Reed Rolf   **Student Consultants**
Sue Dolislager   Fred Dolislager   Carolina Dolislager
Ron Dolislager   Roger Whitehead   Gerrit Dolislager

A BIG thank you to my thorough proofreaders:
Kay Horton   Danelle Scott   Suzanne Kavgian

**Photography and Illustrations
by Marsha Lindenschmidt**

Page x seasons
Page 8 river
Page 9 S-curve
Page 19 church
Page 21 Bible

Page 24 hand with penny
Page 26 Jasmine
Page 29 enhancement
Page 34 Townsend
Page 36 walking

Illustrations by Carolina Dolislager
Page 13 snowman scene
Page 35 skunks

Photography by Kathy Rudd
Page 16 maze — The Netherlands

Marsha giving Carolina art lessons

CONTENTS

Thoughts

on

Nature

Mountain Drama

Spring and summer schedule shows
for which the mountains quit shaving.
Their leafy green beards grow and
begin to hide their craggy faces.

They look forward to these performances.
It's as if they put on disguises
and can tour incognito
as one looks almost like the other.

But each year, autumn
quietly sneaks up on them.
First their leafy costume changes color,
and then it disappears altogether.

When winter arrives,
their true identity is revealed
as their stoic countenance
is dramatically unmasked.

God's annual drama
receives rave reviews each year.

7/07

Their Favorite Time of Year

With smiles on their faces
the trees swayed ever so smugly.
For they were proudly wearing
their new, vivid-green skirts.

Through the long winter months
they'd been forced to wear pants—
dark brown pants—and black pants.
No wonder spring is their favorite season.

5/07

3

The Autumn Gala

The beauty of the dresses threaten
to outshine the backdrop of the mountains' majesty.

The maples twirl in their scarlet red,
vivid orange, and golden yellow frocks.

The oaks waltz about in hues a bit more subdued,
but strong and bold nonetheless.
While the sumac add their surprise moves of crimson.

The vigilant green of the pine trees creates drama.
The sun brings out the best in all of them—
making their dresses sparkle in its sometimes playful spotlight.

The psychedelic splendor is no illusion—
whether on peaks of the mountains,
along the ridges, or in the coves—
their beautiful gowns dominate the scene.

The autumn calendar would be nothing without them.

11/08

Autumn Is All About the Artist

Autumn to me is the fun-loving Artist
setting up His gallery with the game of musical chairs.
When we enter and start playing,
we're content to sit in the first chair we find
and to enjoy the canvas before us.

As the autumn colors change,
it seems like we're witnessing a miracle.
Green turns to yellow, followed by orange and red.
Then the music plays, and it's time to look for another chair.

We grab an open seat, and the canvas before us has a water vista.
The orange-red of the autumn leaves seems to multiply
as they're reflected in the flowing stream.
As the current pulses along, the colors bob up and down enjoying the ride.
Wow! Surely this is the best painting in the show.

Again the music plays.
and a mad free-for-all ensues for a seat.
After much scrambling, we fall into a chair breathing heavily.
Catch your breath. Breathe. Slow your heart rate down.
Now, open your eyes. Wow!

This canvas depicts the Great Smoky Mountains.
The colors are intertwined as many varieties of trees
grow beside one another, up and down the ridges.
But wait, what's that green doing among those vibrant colors?

We see that the Artist has used pine trees as an accent color
to help us appreciate the colorful miracle of autumn.

When the game of musical chairs ends,
we all feel like we are the winners.
We've had a chance to view the Artist's handiwork—
at times up close, and sometimes only quick glimpses.

As we've rushed around in circles,
the experience is indeed phenomenal.

9/07

What's Around the S-Curve?

Between the lazy Townsend Wye and busy Gatlinburg,
twenty miles of S-curves hide and then reveal the wonders of the Smoky Mountains.
The winding and bending of the road closely guard the mountains secrets.
Then . . . suddenly . . . in grand style . . . their beauty is exposed.

One minute the mountains are tall, noncommittal, and sober.
Then . . . around the curve . . . they are playing . . . in the water.
The Little River tumbles over their faces cleaning them up
for their on-going performance for the fortunate visitors.

The next curve finds them once again minding their business:
sustaining the multitude of trees that grow on their slopes.
It takes strong shoulders to hold all that foliage in place,
keeping each tree and fern upright and healthy.

Around another curve, near the river and ravines,
a colorful accent to the tall, green trees appears.
The mountains are wearing skirts . . . of rhododendron,
randomly painted purple and pink and white.

Just as it looks like the vivid display is over, the road curves again,
and the bright orange lilies are producing a riot of random color.
The flowers tickle the mountains in unexpected places,
once again changing their formal façade into a cheerful side show.

The lengthy pageant of the stoic Smoky Mountains
captures and holds our attention along the winding road.
Their ever-changing façade continues to entice us.
We keep driving the S-curves . . . anticipating . . . What's next?

5/12

Haute Couture in East Tennessee

The dogwoods model their pink and white dresses.

The red buds flaunt their new spring apparel.

while the tulips parade in multicolored skirts

and sprightly strut from yard to yard.

Forsythia pose on the hills and the roadsides

where the daffodils wave to us.

One should drive slowly when viewing God's fashion show

that weaves around the mountain and into town.

4/07

A Sunny September Day

Bubbling river . . . Tall, tall trees . . . Waterfalls . . . Friendly folks

. . . a sunny September day in the Smoky Mountains.

9/12/11

Rainy Day Concert

Random keyholes of light intersperse themselves

throughout the green canopy of trees surrounding the log cabin.

Like a thirsty army embracing the long-awaited rain,

the trees reach their arms ever skyward.

Sounds of smiles and gentle waving echo throughout the canopy

as the sprinkles of rain dance and bounce from leaf to leaf.

Thankful for the moisture that helps them achieve their lush green,

they break out in a waltz, gracefully swaying from side to side.

At the same time the rain loudly beats on the nearby steel roof.

"Listen to me—I'm stronger!" the roof taunts the trees.

The lighter melodic notes of the swaying leaves—composed by God,

punctuated by the bass beats from the roof—added by man,

provide a rainy day concert for all . . . on a Monday morning.

6/12

White Magic

The further we drive up the mountain,
the more the snow thickens.

At the various pull-outs
families with young children
are reveling in the white magic.

Snowballs are made and thrown,
accompanied by giggles and high fives.

At the next pull-out,
a snowman stands proudly
as the happy children pose
beside him for a photo.

Snow—another bit of magic
that our mountains
and their Creator give us.

Photo of Phyllis with her
father's Bible, taken in
First Baptist Church of
West Palm Beach, FL, 1991.

*"To me the Bible represents
my heavenly Father's words,
and my earthly father's Bible
carries a special meaning
as he read it every day
for guidance in his life."*

14

Palm Beach Post   Photos by JEFF GREENE/Staff Photo

Thoughts

on

Faith

Lost

Life is full of mazes.

But the Son shows the way—

even when it's dark.

No landmarks . . .

No maps . . .

No drama . . .

Just faith.

2/19/09

Get Out of the Boat

They point their finger at Peter
and loudly proclaim to all,
"He took his eyes off Jesus,
and into the water he went."

But what they neglect to tell us
is that he gave us a great example:
Peter got out of the boat . . .
forsaking the security of what he knew.

We, too, need to trust God for our future
and move out of our comfort zone.
Get out of the boat with Jesus
and gain eternal rewards.

Don't be like the eleven disciples
who hung onto their seats and oars.
Be bold and adventuresome like Peter
and get out of your seat and go.

A chance of a lifetime lies before you:
A chance to live a life of abundance.
It's a lot like walking on water—
a chance to walk by faith.   (Matt. 14: 25-32)   8/07

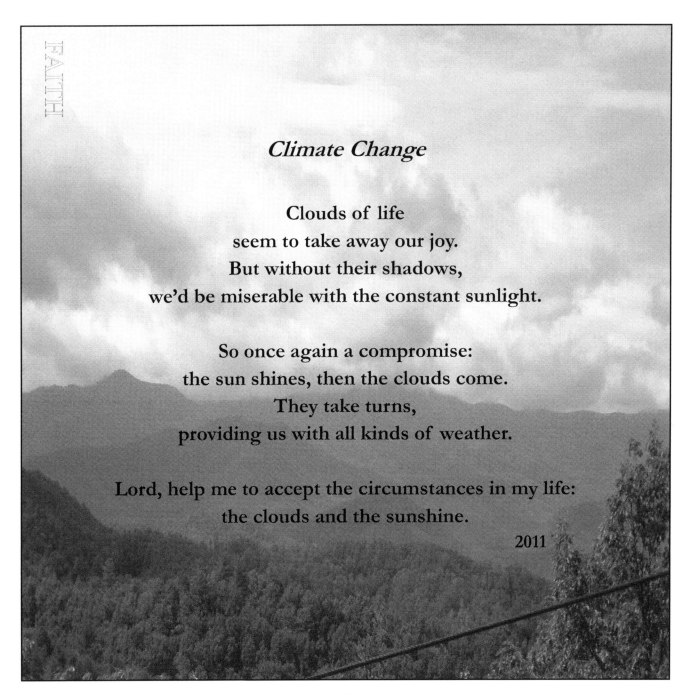

Climate Change

Clouds of life
seem to take away our joy.
But without their shadows,
we'd be miserable with the constant sunlight.

So once again a compromise:
the sun shines, then the clouds come.
They take turns,
providing us with all kinds of weather.

Lord, help me to accept the circumstances in my life:
the clouds and the sunshine.

2011

Reflections
on Visiting Cades Cove

Green, green everywhere—
waiting for the mist to lift—
revealing God's handiwork
to the early and the adventurous visitor.

Hand-made fences encircle the fields
telling a story of a hundred years ago.
Who or what will tell our story
a hundred years from now?

Old churches and the memories they hold—
call to us to make memories of our own.
Thankfully the God they worshipped
still hears and answers our prayers today.

8/07

19

Is This the Time?

All of a sudden I don't want to be left alone.
I've always been strong and independent,
but now I've turned into a weeping wimp.
Why do feelings of weakness bring tears?

Is this just a cycle that I'm going through?
Will my strength and emotions once again plateau?
Or is this the time—the time that it's for real?
Is this the time that my energy doesn't return?

My fear has almost immobilized me.
It's making me cling to my husband—
not wanting him to travel next week.
It's put my mind through countless scenarios.

Will I be strong enough to accept new weakness?
Will my friends stick by me?
Will I have to give up all of my work?
Is God asking me to rely on Him more?

Is this the time
that I put feet to my faith?
Or is this the time
that I wait patiently for God?   9/03

But those who hope in the Lord will renew their strength.
They will soar on wings like eagles; they will run and not grow weary,
they will walk and not be faint.
                    Isaiah 40:31 (NIV)

Thoughts of Despair . . . and Faith

Life is looking downward . . .
into a vortex . . .
spinning counter-clockwise.
Gone is the sun. Gone are the blue skies.
Only gray, stormy clouds remain.

And this vortex
is the sucking kind.
As I lean over to get a better look,
it reaches up . . .
trying to draw me in.

It brings dark thoughts to my mind.
Thoughts of wheelchairs,
mini vans, and lifts.
Thoughts of no longer walking.
Thoughts of dependency and . . . despair.

Where is God in all of this?
Is this His plan?
Would He stoop to this?
Can't He do better?
Doesn't He **need** me to be working?

Or is He trying to get my attention
focused on Him
and His power?
Is He reminding me that
He'll never leave me nor forsake me?

Lord, help me to willingly embrace
the future that You have for me.
Help me to embrace You
and Your will for my life.

I know that you don't **need** me
to accomplish Your agenda.
But *I* need to be willing to accept
Your will for my life.

9/03

A God-Thing at Home Depot

I was looking for a pretty pot
to put flowers in to brighten up our front patio.

I found a beautiful, large, red one at Home Depot . . .
on the top shelf . . . behind some others.
It was the only one of its kind.

I decided to ask an employee the price.
He had to get a ladder. Then I was feeling bad.
I knew it was probably $40 or more—I shouldn't have bothered him.
No way would I pay that much!

Once he reached it and scanned it,
he blinked . . . and shook his head.
Then he announced, "It says . . . it's . . . ONE CENT!"

I said, "SOLD!"
He laughed and said he'd ask his manager.
I wandered down the aisle . . . hopeful . . . doubtful.

When I returned a couple of minutes later,
he was taking the pot off the shelf . . . and he handed it to me.
"The manager says that it's yours!"

WOW! A MIRACLE! I thought.
I said to him, "This is a God-thing."

2/2011

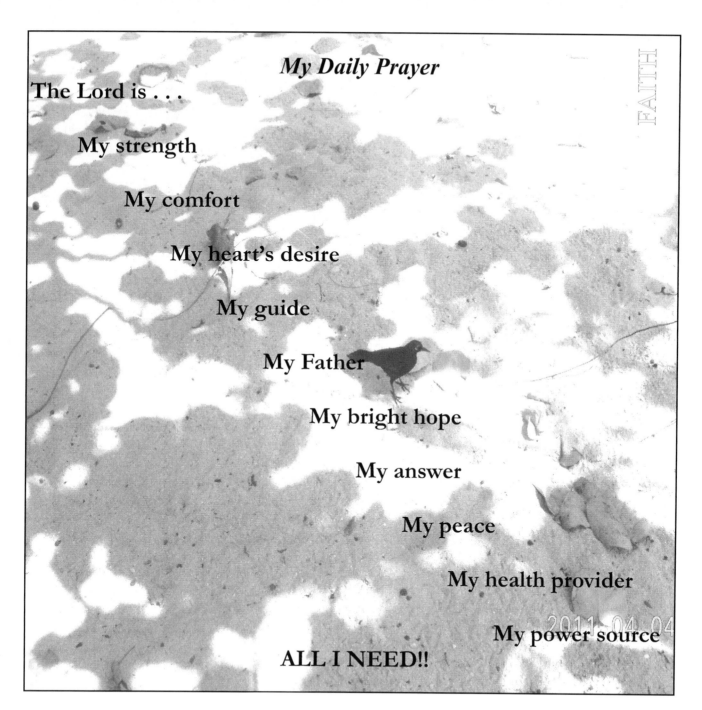

My Daily Prayer

The Lord is . . .

My strength

My comfort

My heart's desire

My guide

My Father

My bright hope

My answer

My peace

My health provider

My power source

ALL I NEED!!

FAITH

2011 04 04

25

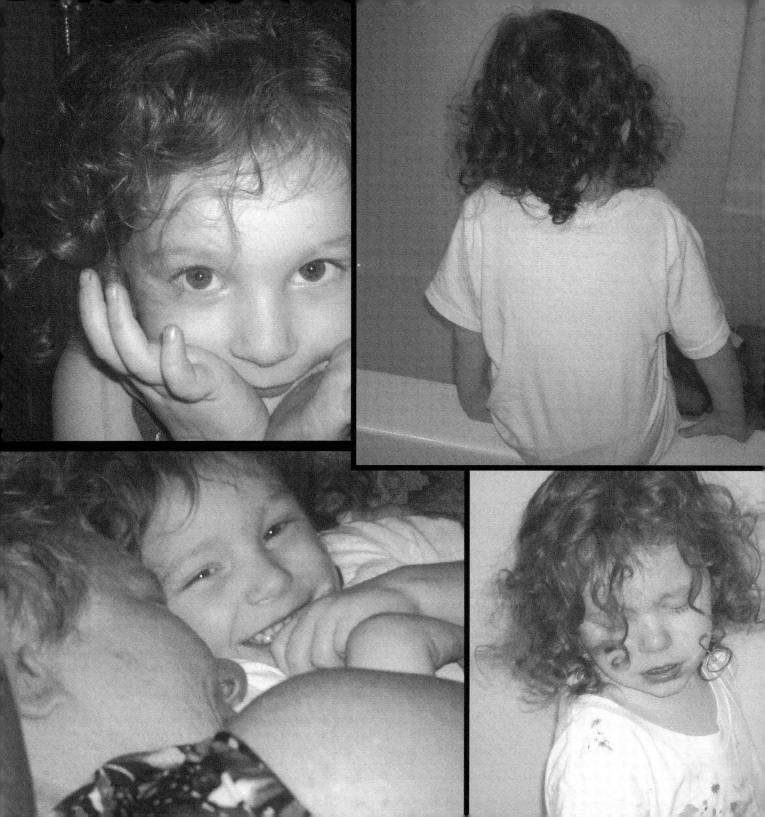

Monday Morning at the River

Taking its own sweet time
The Little River meanders along.
The tree-lined banks gently breathe in
and then expand out again into the water.

Ridges of rocks and stone formations,
along with small rectangle fields of grass,
interrupt—but don't impede its flow.
Its date, with the Tennessee River, will be kept.

Happy to have the sunshine as its companion,
the voice of the river happily bubbles.
Punctuating the morning, a large yellow butterfly
flutters by as two smaller brown ones play tag.

The vista would be great potential for an artist:
blue skies, tree branches trying to touch the water,
rocks piled in a heap at the river's bend—
as sunshine and shadow jump back and forth, changing positions.

But the gentle sounds of the river are drowned out
by the man-made noise of cars and trucks
hastily making their way up and down the highway.
The lawn mower adds its wild bass notes to the raucous tune.

Partially hidden behind a tree, stands a man.
A man—poised—ever watchful, with his fishing pole.
Oblivious to the beauty surrounding him . . .
Oblivious to the harsh, encroaching sounds?

Focused . . . He's focused!
His one immediate goal:
What will be on his dinner plate tonight?
Fresh, fried fish—or a frozen, fish fillet from the store.

05/12

29

Niagara Falls

The small boat shudders
as its wet passengers bounce up and down on the decks.
Even as the cautious sun waves to them,
the plunging water sprays more and more mist.

The intense roar of the cascading water
articulates the vast power it contains.

The blue rain coats seemed to swim on the boat's deck,
but the faces display only awe and wonder
as they stand face to face with
one of the natural wonders of the world.

No experience compares to the journey
to the base of Niagara Falls.
Or is it a physical metaphor
telling the story of our lives?

7/07

Contentment

The mountains don't complain.
They continue to pose for us—
no matter the season,
no matter the weather.

But I wonder . . .
Do they ever wish that they could jump rope
or skip from cove to cove calling,
"You're it," to their nearest neighbor?

Or are they content to sit
with their hands folded in their laps--
an inspiration to all mankind,
who come to gaze on their majesty.

Their silent beauty stretches before us
proclaiming the awesomeness of God.
Oh, that you and I could be more like
the non-complaining mountains.

5/07

Rows of Artwork

From observing rows of corn and ripe, amber wheat in Michigan,
    I moved on to college in another state.

There I was surrounded by rows of stately buildings
    and the largest library I'd ever seen . . .
    with rows upon rows of books to pursue.

Next I embarked upon my first teaching position.
    The rows there were comprised of students sitting at their desks.
    Debate teams and drama productions completed the landscape.

Marriage, too, officially began with rows . . . of pews holding family and friends,
    and a long aisle to walk as I committed my heart to Ron.

Later, motherhood brought diapers, formula, and rows of little-boy toys.
    It also brought new arms to hug and sounds of laughter to savor.

What exhibit would be next?

Thoughts of another continent hadn't been on our radar.
> Everything in Liberia was in random clusters—huts, rice fields, outdoor markets.
> Warm handshakes and savory rice and soup were part of the experience.
> But . . . in the interior . . . rows of rubber trees completed the canvas.

Then we were greeted by the coastal seas of Florida
> and rows of palm trees.
> The tropical landscape was a warm reminder of Africa.

Years later, the rows . . . and peaks . . . of the Smoky Mountains saluted us
> as we moved into their midst.

God's canvases and man's rows of attempted order have been a profound venue.
> We've enjoyed our trip to the best art museums in the world.

10/10

The Outsider

"He married an outsider," she said.
And we all thought she meant
someone from the North or Northeast—
someone who wasn't from the South.

But being curious, we had to ask,
"Where did she come from?"
Imagine our surprise when she replied, "Maryville."
That's just the next town over!

And so it is in Appalachia.
Either you were born and raised here . . .
or you're an outsider.

At first we laughed.
Then we looked around our group,
squirmed in our seats a bit,
remembering . . .
We were all . . . Outsiders.

7/07

*Old-timers remember
Townsend when the main
street was only two lanes.*

Pollution

No matter the glory of the view . . .
the skunk can and will add his unwelcome touch,
making us appreciate . . .
a breath of fresh air.

8/07

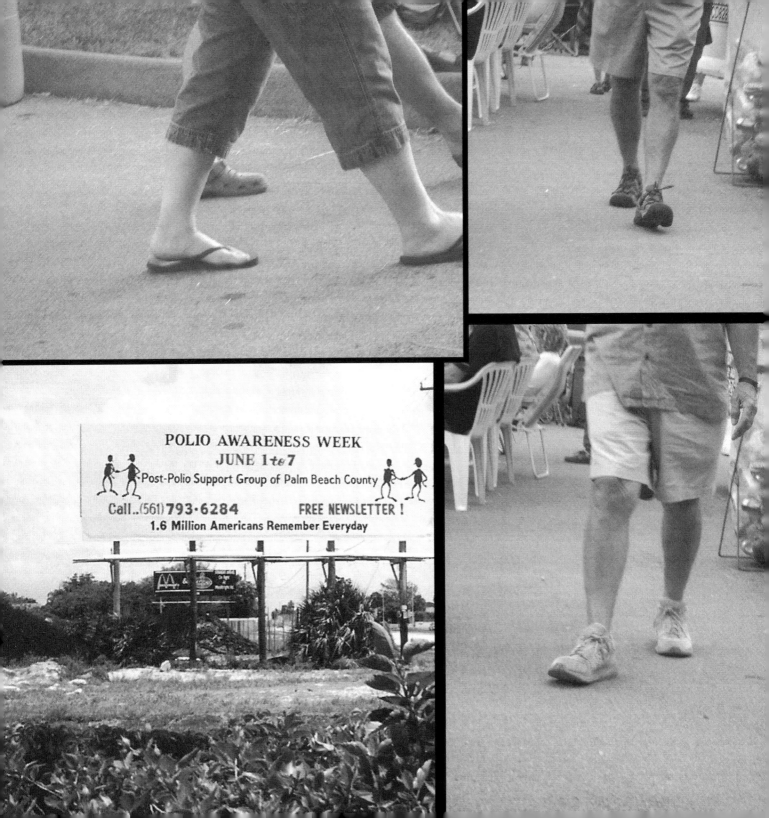

POLIO AWARENESS WEEK
JUNE 1 to 7
Post-Polio Support Group of Palm Beach County
Call..(561) 793·6284   FREE NEWSLETTER !
1.6 Million Americans Remember Everyday

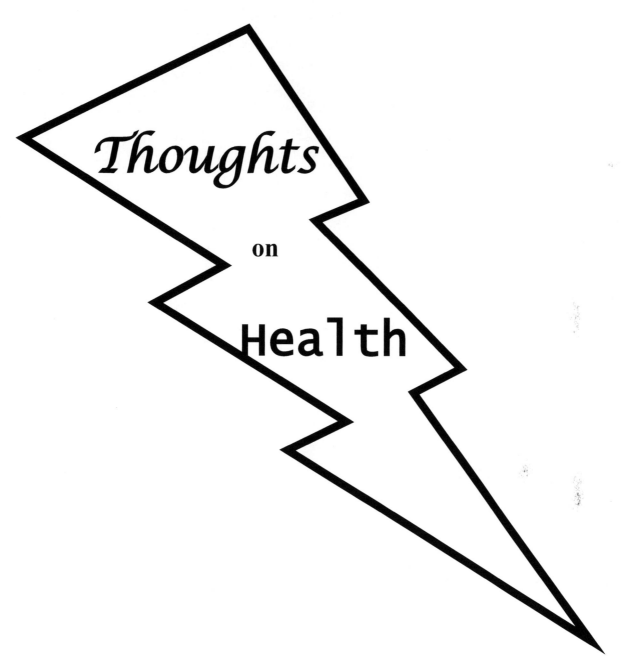

Thoughts on Health

Walking: the Magical Attraction

All of a sudden
I was lying on the bathroom floor.
"Did you faint?" Ron asked.
I really didn't know.
But I did know that I was cold.

As he had helped me out of the tub,
I'd put my weaker foot out first.
And as the rest of me followed . . .
down I went.

Oh, the indignity
to be crumpled on the floor . . .
weak . . . faint . . . cold . . . wet.
I cried.
The leg cramps throughout the night
had foreshadowed this event.
And walking on the uneven ground
at the Spring Festival the evening before
had probably triggered the cramps.

It's back to the power chair
or be prepared to face more indignity.
It really shouldn't be such a difficult decision.
But walking has such a magical attraction . . .
once it's been taken from us.

4/07

Special People

I think there will be a special place in heaven for caregivers.

Have you loaded wheelchairs into cars or vans
or cut up food and gently placed it into your mate's mouth,
or emptied bladder bags or positioned sleep machines?
There must be a special place for you.

Have you stood in line to buy take-out
or stopped for groceries on your way home from work?
There's a special place in our hearts for you.

Have you held the hand of your ill, loved one and reminded them
of why you chose to marry him/her in the first place?
And then added the reasons why you'd do it all over again?
There's a special reward in heaven for you.

You may think that no one knows
and no one cares or understands,
but you're wrong, my friend.

This week hold your head a little higher and
place a smile on your face.
For someone sees your acts of kindness—
He cares, and He remembers.
Show kindness and mercy to one another.
(Zechariah 7:9)   10/03

Wednesday Morning at the Medical Center

Right foot swollen almost two weeks.
"You need an ultrasound of your leg. Go right now."
Paperwork.
Others have their spouses fill it out.
Wonder if they're too nervous to do it themselves.
$30 co-pay.
Need your ID and insurance card.
Sign the disclaimer—2 pages.
What's your email?
Pouring rain. Umbrellas. Worn magazines.
Friendly receptionist. Quiet bookkeeper. Pacing man.
Miss Phyllis . . .
Can't pronounce the last name.
Take off your shorts—cover with the sheet.
Finally . . . .
No blood clots in either leg.
Yea-a-a.
Time for lunch!

3/09

40

We Are Survivors

Inspired by Jody Taylor who said,
"I should have gotten this powered wheelchair two years ago."

Long before we'd heard of body types,
personality profiles, or right brain/left brain—
we finished what we'd begun and always did our best.
Work ethic. We had it.
        We were survivors.

As we grew and matured, no one needed to encourage us.
We gave ourselves more pressure than we could handle.
We were Type A: hard-driving, time-conscious,
overachieving perfectionists.

We personified self-esteem.
We knew all about drive.
        We were survivors.

And then post-polio syndrome reared its ugly head,
and we tasted our first loss of confidence
since contracting polio.

And it was a major loss: our health, our bodies.
We were letting ourselves down: we were failing.

This was a new experience for us.
We didn't know how to handle it.
        We were survivors.

Embrace an assistive device?
Take a nap? Ask for help?
What ridiculous mirage was this!
        We were the survivors—not the losers.

It's taken us time to accept our new limitations.
We'd rather die in battle . . . than give up.

But one by one our Type A personalities have shifted
to the opposite side of our brains.
We decided that if we were going to have a life . . .
        we needed to embrace our naps . . .
                use our assistive devices . . .
                        and once again become survivors.

Now we buy minivans to transport our electric scooters and wheelchairs.
We take vacations on accommodating cruise lines.
And reluctantly we admit how stubborn we'd been not to accept
the help that had been available to us years earlier.

We're still Type A. Our minds haven't stopped working.
But now we're educating our younger doctors . . . about post-polio.
We're striving for enforcement of the [1]ADA.

Thank God, we still have a job to do!
    We are survivors.

10/03

[1] Americans with Disabilities Act

Our Ten Minute Vacation
or
Was It All A Set-Up?

"Amazing Grace how sweet the sound."
I sang the words to that song over and over again.
I couldn't think of anything else to calm my nerves.

I actually remembered three verses.
But when I got to, "When we've been there ten thousand years,"
I paused . . . did this mean I was going to die?

The helicopter wasn't nearly as much fun
as our ride in one had been in St. Augustine for our 40th Anniversary.
But then it had been daylight . . . and Ron was with me . . .
and I wasn't on a medevac flight to Miami.

An hour earlier—911 was called.
I couldn't speak.
We had started to register at Duval House in Key West.
When the clerk asked me questions, I couldn't reply.
She tried three times.

In the ambulance, on the way to the hospital,
I wanted to tell the crew that some people
wouldn't believe that I was speechless.
Me—the talkative one—the speech and drama instructor.

The helicopter was at the hospital waiting . . .
put there by God??
It came for another patient, but they no longer needed it.

As I made the scary trip—
wedged against one side of the helicopter,
lying on a hard board—it felt ominous.
But I prayed.
I reminded God that He could make the time fly—
and He did.

Then I smiled—
I had so wanted Fred and Tom to come for my birthday.
Now when they heard that Mother had a stroke . . .
maybe they'd come out of guilt . . . or duty.
Whatever . . . I'd take it.

Fifty minutes later, we landed in Miami,
and they sent me to the enclosed MRI.
I sang Amazing Grace some more,
and asked God to make the time fly, again.
And He did.

By the time I was in a hospital bed . . .
in the stroke ICU,
my speech had returned.
This time I prayed for Ron.

That morning we'd driven six hours to Key West,
and now he was making the return trip, alone.

This was our shortest vacation ever . . .
about ten minutes.

I thanked God . . .
once again His hand of protection had been on me.
The helicopter was sitting there in Key West . . .waiting for me,
so they could administer t-PA—the clot busting drug,
and get me to a neurologist in Miami, in time to monitor me.

I had packed some books to give away
on our seven-day vacation.
Instead, they went to doctors and nurses,
who aren't used to getting gifts from patients.
They were surprised and pleased.

When I got back to West Palm Beach
and went to see my doctor,
he and his nurses assured me
that God surely was watching over me.

OK, God.
I can lose my speech . . .
be scared in the helicopter and the MRI machine . . .
but my faith is in You! It's in You.
So glad You're always with me.

P.S.
It was a nice finishing touch
arranging for Fred and Tom to come for my birthday
two weeks after this incident.
Thank You!

But . . . next time . . . could You . . . maybe . . .
do something . . . a little less frightening?   11/11

46

Be merciful to me, O God, Be merciful to me! For my soul trusts in You;
And in the shadow of Your wings I will make my refuge.

(Psalm 57:1 KJV)

Celebrating my birthday with sons: Fred and Tom

47

About the Author
Phyllis Porter Dolislager

Phyllis Porter Dolislager was an educator—speech, drama, and writing—most of her life. When post-polio took her out of the classroom, she started writing and giving writing workshops. She is the author of ten books. She and her husband Ron split their time between Tennessee and Florida.

Other books by Phyllis Porter Dolislager that you might enjoy
Who Hit the Down Button? Life with a Chronic Illness or Disability
Lessons Learned on the Farm
A Step Back In Time When Life Was Simpler and Family Was Celebrated

Marsha Lindenschmidt
Creative Consultant

Born a rebel in 1948 and raised in Yankee Land, she worked as an artist in floral design for over 40 years. She didn't begin painting until 1990, when her sister came to Georgia. Her sister had taken drawing classes at a local community college and since Marsha had always wanted to paint, they decided to just do it—paint together. Since that time she has learned by reading, experimenting and art workshops. She has won many awards locally and her works are in collections here and abroad. However, her first love is teaching and sharing with her communities through workshops and art exhibits.

Made in the USA
Columbia, SC
19 February 2022

55995131R00033